WILDFLOWERS

MARFÉ FERGUSON DELANO

All photographs supplied by the
Earth Scenes Division of Animals Animals Enterprises

**NATIONAL
GEOGRAPHIC
SOCIETY**

INTRODUCTION

Wildflowers are among nature's most beautiful gifts. These colorful plants grow almost everywhere, from deserts to swamps, from mountains to fields, from roadsides to city lots.

A wildflower is a plant that can survive without human help. Some are so widespread that they are often called weeds. Some wildflowers are native to North America. That means that they existed here long before humans walked the earth. Other wildflowers were brought here from Europe, Africa, or Asia, but soon spread naturally in their new home.

There are more than 10,000 kinds of wildflowers in North America. This book features 34 that are commonly found in Canada and the United States. It includes stories and legends about the flowers, and gives information about how many of them were once used for food or medicine or magic.

WILDFLOWERS

Consultant: Cristol Fleming
Illustrators: Stephen Wagner, Tim Phelps

Copyright © 1998 by the National Geographic Society

Published by
The National Geographic Society
John M. Fahey, Jr., President and Chief Executive Officer
Gilbert M. Grosvenor, Chairman of the Board
Nina D. Hoffman, Senior Vice President
William R. Gray, Vice President and Director, Book Division

Staff for this Book
Barbara Lalicki, Director of Children's Publishing
Barbara Brownell, Senior Editor and Project Manager
Marianne R. Koszorus, Senior Art Director and Project Manager
Toni Eugene, Editor
Alexandra Littlehales, Art Director
Marfé Ferguson Delano, Writer-Researcher
Susan V. Kelly, Illustrations Editor
Carl Mehler, Senior Map Editor
Jennifer Emmett, Assistant Editor
Mark A. Caraluzzi, Director of Direct Response Marketing
Vincent P. Ryan, Manufacturing Manager
Lewis R. Bassford, Production Project Manager

Visit our Web site at www.nationalgeographic.com

Library of Congress Catalog Card Number: 97-76352
ISBN: 0-7922-3453-7

Color separations by Quad Graphics, Martinsburg, West Virginia
Printed in Mexico by R.R. Donnelly & Sons Company

Some wildflowers are poisonous, so never eat any of them. Do not pick them either. Insects and animals depend on them for food. Some wildflowers are rare, mostly because their habitats have been destroyed by development.

HOW TO USE THIS BOOK

The wildflowers in this book are organized by four habitats. First come woodland wildflowers, then grassland, desert, and wetland. Each spread helps you to identify one kind of flower. It gives you information about the plant's size, appearance, when it blooms, and more. A shaded map shows where the plant grows in Canada and the United States, and the "Field Notes" entry gives an interesting fact about it. If you find a word you do not know, look it up in the Glossary on page 76.

PARTS OF A FLOWER

Although wildflowers may look very different from each other, they all have some parts in common, and they all have the same job. This job is to produce seeds from which new plants can grow. Every flower has male parts, called stamens, and female parts, called pistils. Stamens produce fine powdery grains called pollen. At the base of the pistil is a swelling called the ovary, where the seeds will grow.

Stamens and pistils are surrounded by petals, the colorful parts of a flower that attract insects. Small, leaf-like sepals, which are usually green, form a ring below the petals.

Pollen may be carried from the stamen of one flower to the pistil of another by the wind or by creatures exploring the blossoms for pollen or nectar. This transferring of pollen is called pollination, and it causes the seeds to develop in the ovary. As the seeds grow, the ovary around them gradually forms into a fruit.

stamen

pistil

ovary

sepal

petal

leaf

stem/stalk

7

VIOLET

This little flower has been a favorite since ancient times, when it was used for decorating homes and making medicines. In the spring, look for violets pushing up through the dead leaves on the forest floor.

○○○○○○○○○○○○○
FIELD NOTES
North America has about 80 kinds of violets. Many yellow varieties grow on the West Coast.

By midsummer, the heart-shaped leaves of this common blue violet can grow to be five inches across.

WHERE TO FIND:
These low-growing flowers thrive in wooded areas and moist meadows across Canada and the U.S.

WHAT TO LOOK FOR:

✳ SIZE
The majority of violets grow between three and ten inches tall.

✳ APPEARANCE
Most violets are a shade of purple; some are yellow or white. Flowers have five petals. Leaves are heart-shaped.

✳ FLOWERING
Violets bloom in spring and summer.

✳ MORE
The sweet-smelling oil from some types of violets is used in making perfume.

TRILLIUM

Trilliums are also called wake-robins because many of them bloom in early spring, about the time robins arrive. All trilliums are beautiful, but a few varieties have an unpleasant smell.

FIELD NOTES
A red trillium looks pretty, but smells like rotten meat. This odor draws flies, which pollinate the plant.

Blossoms of the large-flowered trillium gleam like stars in the woods.

WHERE TO FIND:
Trilliums grow along the banks of streams and in woods in both mountains and lowlands.

WHAT TO LOOK FOR:

✳ SIZE
Trilliums grow about 8 to 18 inches tall.

✳ APPEARANCE
Their flowers range from white to pink to maroon. Each has three petals and rises on a stalk above three leaves.

✳ FLOWERING
Trilliums bloom in the spring.

✳ MORE
Trillium roots were once used to treat rattlesnake bites.

WILD GERANIUM

 Also called cranesbill, wild geraniums have long been valued for more than their delicate beauty. Indians and pioneers used the plant to make medicines to treat toothaches and other ailments.

WHERE TO FIND:
Wild geraniums are common in open woods and shady spots across much of Canada and the U.S.

WHAT TO LOOK FOR:

✳ **SIZE**
Wild geraniums grow about one to two feet tall.

✳ **APPEARANCE**
They have pink or purplish flowers that have five petals.

✳ **FLOWERING**
They bloom in spring and summer.

✳ **MORE**
When wild geranium seedpods ripen, they pop open and shoot seeds more than 30 feet into the air.

FIELD NOTES

Similar in shape to a crane's beak, the seedpods of the wild geranium give it its common name, cranesbill.

Wild geraniums have hairy stems and deeply cut leaves.

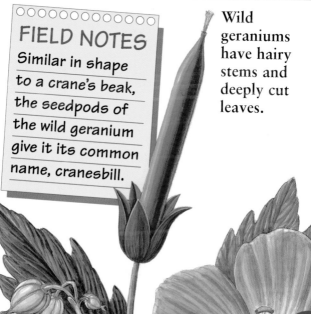

13

JACK-IN-THE-PULPIT

This unusual looking wild-flower gets its name from its shape, which resembles a figure—called Jack—standing in a pulpit, or preacher's stand. Native Americans gathered its roots as a vegetable.

The curving hood of the Jack-in-the-pulpit acts as an umbrella for the flowers hidden deep inside it.

FIELD NOTES

In the fall, a Jack-in-the-pulpit bears a cluster of tightly-packed red berries where its flowers once grew.

WHERE TO FIND:
You can find Jack-in-the-pulpits nestled in moist woods and swamps from Nova Scotia to Texas.

WHAT TO LOOK FOR:

✳ **SIZE**
This plant grows one to two feet tall.

✳ **APPEARANCE**
The curving hood of this wildflower is green or purplish brown, and may be striped. It surrounds a green or brown club-shaped spike.

✳ **FLOWERING**
Jack-in-the-pulpits bloom in spring.

✳ **MORE**
The tiny flowers of this plant are hidden inside, at the base of the spike.

COLUMBINE

This wildflower looks like a tiny flock of fluttering doves to some people. That is why it was named columbine, from the Latin word for "dove." A myth says that lions ate this wildflower to gain strength.

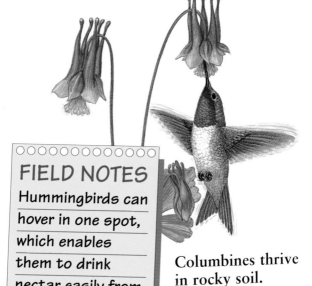

FIELD NOTES

Hummingbirds can hover in one spot, which enables them to drink nectar easily from a columbine.

Columbines thrive in rocky soil. These wildflowers are also called rock bells.

WHAT TO LOOK FOR:

✳ SIZE
Columbines grow one to two feet tall.

✳ APPEARANCE
The most common columbine has red-and-yellow flowers that dangle upside down from long slender stems. The leaves are deeply cut.

✳ FLOWERING
It blooms in spring and summer.

✳ MORE
Some columbines are blue. They bloom in aspen groves in the Rockies.

LADY'S SLIPPER

With its distinctive shape and bright color, this wildflower attracts many passing bees. Insects enter the wildflower through an opening at its top, but the exit is through a tiny hole at the back.

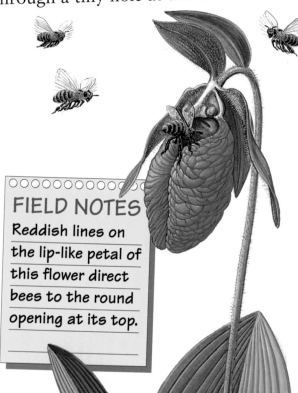

FIELD NOTES

Reddish lines on the lip-like petal of this flower direct bees to the round opening at its top.

WHAT TO LOOK FOR:

✳ SIZE
The pink lady's slipper grows 6 to 15 inches tall.

✳ APPEARANCE
It has a pouch-shaped, rosy pink flower on a leafless stalk.

✳ FLOWERING
It blooms from April through July.

✳ MORE
Another common lady's slipper has one or two yellow flowers on a leafy stalk. It grows taller than its pink cousin.

Also known as the moccasin flower, lady's slipper gets both of its names from its shoe-like shape.

JACOB'S LADDER

Unlike many wildflowers, Jacob's ladder gets its name from its leaves, not its blossoms. The name refers to a Bible story in which a man named Jacob dreams he sees a ladder to heaven.

FIELD NOTES

The flowers of this plant nod when in bud and straighten up as they open.

The paired leaflets of Jacob's ladder look somewhat like the rungs of a miniature ladder.

WHERE TO FIND:
These plants grow in woodlands and mountain forests in eastern and western Canada and the U.S.

WHAT TO LOOK FOR:

✳ SIZE
Jacob's ladder grows about one to three feet tall.

✳ APPEARANCE
It has blue or bluish-purple bell-shaped flowers that bloom on leafy stems.

✳ FLOWERING
Jacob's ladder blooms in spring and summer.

✳ MORE
Jacob's ladder sometimes grows in marshy fields and along stream banks.

SPRING BEAUTY

Spring beauty is a sweet-smelling wildflower that barely waits for the snow to melt before bursting into bloom. This delicate-looking plant grows from thick underground stems called tubers.

FIELD NOTES

Indians dug up spring beauty plants and ate the tubers, which look like small potatoes.

Spring beauty blossoms open in sunshine. They close on cloudy days.

WHAT TO LOOK FOR:

✳ SIZE
Spring beauty grows about 6 to 12 inches tall.

✳ APPEARANCE
The flowers have pink or white petals with darker pink veins. They bloom in a cluster above a pair of long leaves.

✳ FLOWERING
Spring beauty plants bloom from about March to June.

✳ MORE
Deer graze on spring beauty plants.

23

WOOD ANEMONE

 Wood anemones (uh-NEH-muh-neez) are also called windflowers because the slightest breeze sets them dancing. The flower's stalk is so thin and flexible that it bends and sways easily.

WHERE TO FIND:

Wood anemones, which grow in open woods and hillsides, are often found around the roots of trees.

WHAT TO LOOK FOR:

✳ SIZE
The plant grows 6 to 12 inches tall.

✳ COLOR
Wood anemones have a single white flower that blooms on a slender stalk above three leaves.

✳ FLOWERING
The plant flowers from April to June.

✳ MORE
Native Americans in Canada made tea from wood anemones and used the brew to treat a variety of illnesses.

The undersides of wood anemone blossoms are often pink.

BLACK-EYED SUSAN

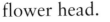 The "eye," or center, of this wildflower is really brown.

It is made up of hundreds of tiny flowers. The parts that look like petals are called rays. Together the flowers and rays are called the flower head.

FIELD NOTES

Like natural bird feeders, black-eyed Susans offer goldfinches hundreds of tiny, tasty seeds.

Black-eyed Susan plants like these are used to make green and yellow dyes.

WHERE TO FIND:
Native to the prairie, black-eyed Susans now grow along roadsides and in fields from coast to coast.

WHAT TO LOOK FOR:

✳ SIZE
Black-eyed Susan grows one to three feet tall.

✳ APPEARANCE
It has yellow flower heads with brown centers. The leaves are long and fuzzy.

✳ FLOWERING
It blooms from June through October.

✳ MORE
Black-eyed Susan stems have tiny bristles that discourage unwanted pests, such as ants, from climbing the plants.

INDIAN PAINTBRUSH

GRASSLAND

 Indian paintbrush blazes with bright, brilliant color. These hues are not from its blossoms—which are tiny and plain—but from small leaves called bracts that surround the flowers.

WHERE TO FIND:
Indian paintbrush grows in meadows and prairies and along roadsides from coast to coast.

WHAT TO LOOK FOR:

✱ **SIZE**
The plant grows one to three feet tall.

✱ **APPEARANCE**
The flower head of this plant looks like a ragged brush dipped in red, yellow, or orange paint.

✱ **FLOWERING**
It blooms in late spring and summer.

✱ **MORE**
Indians used concoctions made from this wildflower to soothe burned skin.

Indian paintbrush plants glow like
crimson flames on the prairie.

FIREWHEEL

Firewheels grow in large patches that spread over the prairie like huge carpets. This plant is also called blanket flower, because the colors and patterns of its blooms resemble those of Indian blankets.

WHERE TO FIND:
You can find firewheel plants growing in sandy plains, prairies, deserts, and along roadsides.

WHAT TO LOOK FOR:

✳ SIZE
A firewheel plant usually grows one to two feet tall.

✳ APPEARANCE
It has red rays tipped with yellow. The leaves are long and fuzzy.

✳ FLOWERING
Firewheels bloom from May to July.

✳ MORE
Firewheels withstand heat and dryness and thrive in poor soil. Some firewheels in the Southwest are all yellow.

A moth caterpillar rests on the tiny flowers that make up the center of a firewheel blossom.

BUTTERCUP

 Buttercups grow all over the world. You may even find some in your own yard. Be careful not to crush a buttercup. The plant contains a bitter juice that can irritate your skin.

WHERE TO FIND:
Buttercups grow from coast to coast in fields and meadows. They thrive in moist locations.

WHAT TO LOOK FOR:

✳ **SIZE**
Buttercups grow two to three feet tall.

✳ **APPEARANCE**
Buttercups have glossy yellow flowers with five petals. The stems are hairy and the leaves have many points.

✳ **FLOWERING**
This wildflower blooms from April through July.

✳ **MORE**
The shiny surface of buttercup petals helps attract passing insects.

The buttercup got its name from the color and shape of its blossoms.

FIELD NOTES

Cows grazing in fields avoid eating buttercups because of this wildflower's bitter taste.

BUTTER-AND-EGGS

Originally brought to North America by colonists from Europe, this wildflower is named for its two-toned blossoms. The yellow is the color of butter, and the orange is the shade of egg yolks.

Another name for this flower is toadflax because the orange parts look somewhat like the mouth of a toad.

WHERE TO FIND:
This wildflower grows in thick patches along roads, in fields, and in vacant lots from coast to coast.

WHAT TO LOOK FOR:

✸ SIZE
It grows one to three feet tall.

✸ APPEARANCE
A butter-and-eggs plant has yellow and orange flowers that grow in a cluster on an erect, leafy stem.

✸ FLOWERING
It blooms from July through October.

✸ MORE
Early colonists in North America used butter-and-eggs to make a medicine to treat sore throats.

FIELD NOTES
The lip-like orange petals of this flower show the hawkmoth where to dip its tongue for nectar.

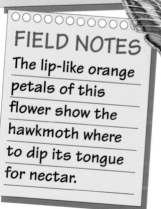

GOLDENROD

This handsome wildflower is a favorite hangout of the praying mantis. The large green insect perches on the flower's stems and waits to nab the many flying insects drawn to its golden blossoms.

FIELD NOTES

In the fall, the praying mantis often lays its eggs on this plant. The eggs hatch in spring.

Colonists brewed a kind of tea with goldenrod plants like these blooming in a field.

WHERE TO FIND:
Goldenrod flowers decorate fields and roadsides across Canada and throughout the United States.

WHAT TO LOOK FOR:

✳ SIZE
Goldenrod grows one to five feet tall.

✳ APPEARANCE
Tiny yellow flower heads grow in clusters on arching stems.

✳ FLOWERING
The plant blooms from July through October.

✳ MORE
Many people blame their allergies on goldenrod. The real culprit is ragweed, which blooms around the same time.

CHICORY

Chicory blooms are often the only splashes of blue among roadside wildflowers. In many places, the plant is prized for its roots, which are roasted, ground, and made into a coffee-like drink.

FIELD NOTES
Thousands of years ago, ancient Egyptians enjoyed a drink made from roasted chicory roots.

Chicory blossoms usually open in the morning and wilt by midday.

WHERE TO FIND:
Chicory plants grow on roadsides and in fields and vacant lots across Canada and throughout the U.S.

WHAT TO LOOK FOR:

✳ SIZE
A chicory plant grows one to five feet tall.

✳ APPEARANCE
It has sky-blue to violet flower heads on branching, erect stems.

✳ FLOWERING
This wildflower blooms from summer through early fall.

✳ MORE
Some Native Americans used to chew the fresh roots of chicory like gum.

QUEEN ANNE'S LACE

The name of this common wildflower comes from its frilly blossoms, which look like lace fit for a queen. Despite its delicate beauty, this deep-rooted plant can be a tough, pesky weed in farmland.

FIELD NOTES

After a flower cluster of Queen Anne's lace dies, it curls up and looks like a tiny bird's nest.

A swallowtail butterfly is one of many insects drawn to this flower's mass of blossoms.

WHAT TO LOOK FOR:

✳ SIZE
This plant grows one to four feet tall.

✳ APPEARANCE
It has hairy stalks topped with clusters of dainty white flowers. The leaves are feathery.

✳ FLOWERING
It blooms from summer to early fall.

✳ MORE
It is the wild ancestor of the carrots we grow in gardens and buy at the market.

WILD BERGAMOT

A member of the mint family, this wildflower was valued by Indians for its aromatic leaves, which were used to make tea. Early colonists also drank bergamot tea as a substitute for imported tea.

A field of wild bergamot fills the air around it with a rich, minty fragrance.

WHERE TO FIND:
Wild bergamot plants grow in sunny fields and meadows in Canada and the U.S.

WHAT TO LOOK FOR:

✳ SIZE
Wild bergamot grows about two to four feet tall.

✳ APPEARANCE
It has globe-like clusters of tube-shaped lavender or pink flowers that grow at the top of hairy stems.

✳ FLOWERING
It blooms June through September.

✳ MORE
The slender blossoms of wild bergamot perfectly fit the hummingbird's bill.

FIELD NOTES
Indians applied fresh, crushed bergamot leaves to their skin to ease the pain of insect bites.

43

FIREWEED

After a fire, this beautiful wild-flower is one of the first plants to spring up through the blackened earth. Even after its top is burned off, fireweed survives, thanks to its tough, hardy root system.

FIELD NOTES

Fireweed was the first plant to bloom in areas devastated by the 1980 eruption of Mount St. Helens.

Fireweed plants often grow in thick patches.

WHERE TO FIND:
This sun-loving wildflower grows in clearings and burned-over areas from coast to coast.

WHAT TO LOOK FOR:

✷ SIZE
Fireweed grows two to six feet tall.

✷ APPEARANCE
It has rose pink, spike-like clusters of flowers that bloom at the top of tall, leafy stems.

✷ FLOWERING
It blooms June through September.

✷ MORE
Indians of the Pacific Northwest used the strong fibers inside fireweed stems to make fishnets and twine.

MILKWEED

Monarch butterfly caterpillars eat the leaves of this wildflower, which gets its name from the milky liquid inside its stems. This juice makes both the caterpillars and the adult butterflies taste bad to birds.

FIELD NOTES

Monarchs lay their eggs on milkweed leaves. The adult butterflies feed on the flowers' nectar.

These milkweed blossoms will be replaced by seedpods that open in the fall.

WHERE TO FIND:
Look for milkweed plants in old fields and along roadsides across much of Canada and the U.S.

WHAT TO LOOK FOR:

❋ SIZE
Milkweeds grow two to six feet tall.

❋ APPEARANCE
The plant has clusters of tiny reddish-pink to purple flowers on sturdy stems.

❋ FLOWERING
It blooms June through August.

❋ MORE
Early settlers in the American Colonies used the sticky white juice inside milkweed plants as a glue.

OXEYE DAISY

The oxeye daisy came to North America when its seeds were accidentally mixed in with crop seeds or animal feed brought here by European colonists. The newcomer soon spread across the land.

FIELD NOTES

Because its yellow center resembles the sun, this flower became known as a "day's eye," or daisy.

Farmers have called the oxeye "whiteweed," because it took over their fields.

WHAT TO LOOK FOR:

✳ SIZE
The oxeye daisy grows one to three feet tall.

✳ APPEARANCE
An oxeye daisy has white flower heads with yellow centers, which grow at the end of slender stems.

✳ FLOWERING
This wildflower blooms all summer.

✳ MORE
The stems and blossoms of oxeye daisies were once used to make hand lotion.

LUPINE

 Lupine gets its name from the Latin word for wolf, "lupus." People once thought that the plant robbed soil of nutrients, just as wolves steal sheep. We now know that lupines actually enrich the soil.

WHERE TO FIND:
Look for these beautiful blue wildflowers in fields, dry plains, and areas with sandy soil.

WHAT TO LOOK FOR:

✹ **SIZE**
Most lupines grow one to two feet tall.

✹ **APPEARANCE**
Lupines have deep blue or violet blossoms that bloom in clusters atop a straight stem.

✹ **FLOWERING**
Most lupines bloom in April to July.

✹ **MORE**
Lupine is a member of the pea family of plants. Its relatives include peanuts, beans, peas, clover, and alfalfa.

Indian legend says that Texas lupines, also called bluebonnets, grew in fields wherever buffalo roamed.

Lupine leaves turn toward the sun during the day and curl up tightly at night.

BLAZING STAR

This wildflower's brightly colored blossoms gave it its name, blazing star. Plains Indians used the roots of blazing star to treat snakebites and sore throats.

WHERE TO FIND:
Blazing star plants grow east of the Rocky Mountains in open places, especially in prairies.

WHAT TO LOOK FOR:

✳ **SIZE**
It grows one to six feet tall.

✳ **APPEARANCE**
Blazing star has feathery clusters of rose pink or purple flowers on top of a tall, stiff stem.

✳ **FLOWERING**
It blooms from late summer through early fall.

✳ **MORE**
The roots of some types of blazing star reach 16 feet into the soil.

The wispy blossoms of blazing star give it its other common name, gayfeather.

FIELD NOTES

Indians fed blazing star flowers to their horses in the belief that they made the animals run faster.

GOLD POPPY

Legend has it that a California hillside once shone so brightly with gold poppies that ships could see it from 25 miles out at sea. The flower's spicy fragrance attracts beetles to its blossoms.

The gold poppy plant opens its petals only in full sunlight and closes them at night.

WHERE TO FIND:
Gold poppies can be found in open areas and deserts in California and the Southwest.

WHAT TO LOOK FOR:

✳ SIZE
This wildflower grows about 8 to 24 inches tall.

✳ APPEARANCE
It has bright goldish orange, cup-shaped flowers that grow at the end of long stalks.

✳ FLOWERING
It blooms from February to September.

✳ MORE
Indians in California once used gold poppy roots to ease toothache pain.

FIELD NOTES

Ablaze with poppies, the California coast was called the "land of fire" by Spanish sailors.

GLOBEMALLOW

This tough but beautiful plant can survive long periods without rain. It is also known as "sore-eye poppy," because the fine hairs on its leaves were thought by some desert people to irritate the eye.

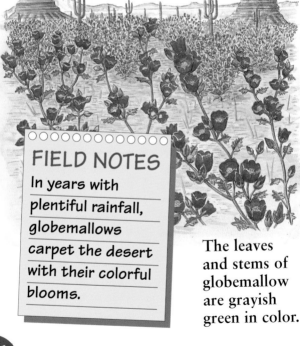

FIELD NOTES

In years with plentiful rainfall, globemallows carpet the desert with their colorful blooms.

The leaves and stems of globemallow are grayish green in color.

WHERE TO FIND:
Globemallows are common in the deserts of southern California and the Southwest.

WHAT TO LOOK FOR:

✳ SIZE
It grows one to five feet tall.

✳ APPEARANCE
Globemallow has bright orange-red or pinkish cup-shaped flowers that grow on woody stems.

✳ FLOWERING
This plant blooms from March through October.

✳ MORE
Some globemallows have as many as 100 stems growing from a single root.

PRICKLY PEAR

This member of the cactus family is covered with spines. It also has tiny, prickly bristles that are hard to see and are painful to the touch. The plant is named for its pear-shaped fruit.

WHERE TO FIND:
Prickly pears grow in deserts and in other sandy or rocky places in much of the United States.

WHAT TO LOOK FOR:

＊ SIZE
Eastern varieties of prickly pear grow about eight inches tall. Western species may reach three to five feet.

＊ APPEARANCE
This plant has flat, spiny, paddle-like stems and bright yellow flowers.

＊ FLOWERING
It blooms in spring and summer.

＊ MORE
Like all cactuses, prickly pears store food and water in their thick pads.

The reddish fruits of prickly pears, also called Indian figs, were used by Indians as food.

The sharp spines on prickly pears help protect them from hungry animals.

MARIPOSA LILY

The large and lovely blossoms of this graceful desert wildflower look to some people like fluttering butterflies. That is how it got its name. The word "mariposa" is Spanish for "butterfly."

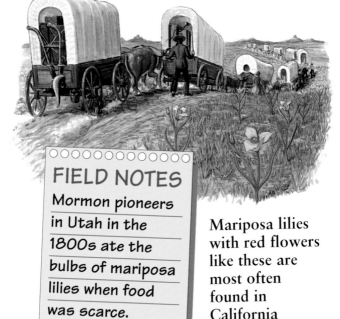

FIELD NOTES

Mormon pioneers in Utah in the 1800s ate the bulbs of mariposa lilies when food was scarce.

Mariposa lilies with red flowers like these are most often found in California and Arizona.

WHERE TO FIND:
This western plant grows in the sandy dry soil of desert foothills, plains, and open forests.

WHAT TO LOOK FOR:

✳ **SIZE**
This wildflower grows about one foot tall.

✳ **APPEARANCE**
It has grass-like leaves. Its tulip-shaped flowers range in color from white to lilac, yellow, orange, and red.

✳ **FLOWERING**
It blooms in late spring and summer.

✳ **MORE**
Mariposa lilies grow from underground bulbs about the size of walnuts.

SEASHORE MALLOW

This wetland wildflower is a cousin of the marshmallow, a plant whose roots were once used to make the candy of the same name. Also known as the saltmarsh mallow, this plant is native to North America.

FIELD NOTES

Like its cousin the marshmallow, the seashore mallow thrives in marshy areas near the ocean.

A seashore mallow looks as if it has a long yellow nose.

WHERE TO FIND:
The seashore mallow grows in salt marshes along the coastline from New York to Texas.

WHAT TO LOOK FOR:

✳ SIZE
A seashore mallow plant grows one to four feet tall.

✳ APPEARANCE
A large plant with rough, gray-green leaves, the seashore mallow has pink flowers with yellow stamens.

✳ FLOWERING
It blooms between May and October.

✳ MORE
The seashore mallow is a relative of the cotton plant.

MARSH MARIGOLD

Gleaming like gold along streams and in swampy woods, the marsh marigold has long been a symbol of spring. People in Europe once decorated the doorways of their cottages with this flower.

FIELD NOTES

The marsh marigold prefers wet soil. These plants can even grow in the middle of a stream.

Hundreds of years ago, marsh marigold blossoms like these were used to make a variety of medicines.

WHAT TO LOOK FOR:

✳ SIZE
The marsh marigold grows one to two feet tall.

✳ APPEARANCE
It has glossy, heart-shaped leaves and shiny yellow flowers.

✳ FLOWERING
It blooms from April to June.

✳ MORE
Native Americans boiled leaves of marsh marigolds and ate them as a vegetable. The raw leaves are poisonous.

CATTAIL

 Cattails have grown on earth since the time of the dinosaurs. Their long leaves shelter animals. Indians made flour from roots. They also boiled the flower spikes and ate them as we eat corn on the cob.

WHERE TO FIND:
Cattails grow in ditches, freshwater marshes and other wet areas across Canada and the U.S.

WHAT TO LOOK FOR:

✳ **SIZE**
This plant grows three to nine feet tall.

✳ **APPEARANCE**
It has sword-like leaves and a spike of tiny yellow flowers atop a sausage-shaped cluster of small brown flowers.

✳ **FLOWERING**
Cattails blossom from May to July.

✳ **MORE**
After blooming, the yellow flowers wither away, leaving the top of the stalk bare.

The long, narrow leaves of cattails can be woven into baskets and mats.

FIELD NOTES

The red-winged blackbird and many other wetland birds roost in patches of cattails.

JOE-PYE WEED

According to legend, this wild-flower is named after an Indian medicine man named Joe Pye, who lived in colonial New England. Joe Pye is said to have used a potion made from this plant to treat fevers.

FIELD NOTES

Also called "queen of the meadow," this plant towers over deer and most other wildlife in wetlands.

When Joe-Pye weed blooms, it is a sign that fall is on the way.

WHERE TO FIND:
Joe-Pye weed grows in damp meadows and along the banks of streams and rivers.

WHAT TO LOOK FOR:

✳ **SIZE**
Joe-Pye weed grows at least two to six feet tall.

✳ **APPEARANCE**
It has clusters of tiny purplish pink flowers on top of tall, thick stems.

✳ **FLOWERING**
It blooms July through September.

✳ **MORE**
Ojibwa Indians believed that washing children in a mixture made from Joe-Pye weed would make them strong.

CARDINAL FLOWER

Like the songbird of the same name, the cardinal flower was named for its fire-engine red color. It is the same shade of red as the robes worn for centuries by religious leaders called cardinals.

FIELD NOTES

The tube-shaped blossoms of the cardinal flower are a perfect match for the long bill of a hummingbird.

Native to North America, the bright red cardinal flower became popular in European gardens.

WHERE TO FIND:
The cardinal flower grows by streams and in other wet places in southern Canada and much of the U.S.

WHAT TO LOOK FOR:

✳ SIZE
The cardinal flower grows two to four feet tall.

✳ APPEARANCE
It has long clusters of brilliant red flowers on straight, leafy stems.

✳ FLOWERING
It blooms from July to September.

✳ MORE
Native Americans once used the root of the cardinal flower to make love charms.

MONKEYFLOWER

With a little imagination, it is easy to see how this wildflower, which favors stream banks and damp meadows, got its name. Its brightly colored blossom looks like the grinning face of a monkey.

FIELD NOTES

Like the inchworm on this plant, monkeyflower blossoms are only about one inch across.

Monkeyflowers in the West have yellow blooms; those in the East have purplish blue blossoms.

WHERE TO FIND:
Monkeyflowers grow in wet places throughout much of Canada and the United States.

WHAT TO LOOK FOR:

✳ **SIZE**
It grows one to three feet tall.

✳ **APPEARANCE**
The flower of the plant is tube-shaped with five petals. It ranges in color from yellow to pink to purplish blue.

✳ **FLOWERING**
It blooms from June to September.

✳ **MORE**
Indians and early settlers in the Rocky Mountains ate monkeyflower leaves as salad greens.

WILD BLUE IRIS

 Also known as blue flag, this wildflower is native to North American wetlands. Other kinds of irises grow in Europe. These colorful flowers were named for Iris, the Greek goddess of the rainbow.

WHERE TO FIND:
Wild blue irises adorn swamps, moist meadows, and other wet areas across Canada and the U.S.

WHAT TO LOOK FOR:

✷ SIZE
Wild blue irises grow between one and three feet tall.

✷ APPEARANCE
It has violet-blue flowers and long, thick, grass-like leaves.

✷ FLOWERING
It blooms from May through August.

✷ MORE
Black dye as well as ink were once made from iris roots.

FIELD NOTES

The roots of some types of irises are used to give a sweet smell to perfumes and to soaps.

Wild blue irises thrive in moist meadows, such as this one in the Rocky Mountains.

GLOSSARY

bract A kind of leaf that grows just below the flower of a plant.

bulb The round, firm, underground stem of some plants.

desert A place where it rarely rains.

flower head A group of small flowers in a tight cluster that are so arranged as to look like a single flower.

fruit A plant's ripened ovary. It holds the seeds of a plant.

grassland Open land with grass growing on it.

habitat The place where a plant or animal is normally found.

marsh A wetland filled with grasses and other small plants.

meadow An open area with flowers and grasses and only a few trees.

ovary The bottom part of a flower's pistil where plant seeds form.

pistil The female part of a flower.

prairie A huge area of grassland.

ray One of the petal-like parts that encircle the centers of some flowers.

salt marsh A marsh that is often covered with seawater.

seed The part of a flower that can grow into a new plant.

seedpod A dry, shell-like fruit that holds the seeds of a plant.

sepal The part of a plant that grows just outside the petals and covers the flower before it blooms.

stamen The male part of a flower.

swamp A wetland with many trees and shrubs.

tuber The thick, underground stem of some plants.

wetland A wet area, such as a moist meadow, marsh, or swamp.

woodland A place with many trees.

INDEX OF
WILDFLOWERS